Devil!

GET YOUR HANDS OFF!

6 Strategies To Snatch Your Kids Out of Deception

Cathy Coppola

ISBN: 978-1530872084

DEDICATION

I dedicate this book to parents who refuse to
allow the current culture to be the defining
voice in their loved ones lives. I believe that the
power of the Word of God will echo in your
heart and cause you to rise up and take back
what the enemy stole from you.

And I also say to you that you are Peter, and on this rock I will build My church, and the gates of Hell shall not prevail against it. And I will give you the keys of the Kingdom of Heaven, and whatever you bind on earth will be bound in heaven, and whatever you loose on earth will be loosed in heaven.

Matthew 16:18 & 19

TABLE OF CONTENTS

NOTE FROM THE AUTHOR

There are two kingdoms in this world, the Kingdom of God and the Kingdom of Satan. The Kingdom of God resides on earth within the heart of each believer in Jesus Christ. As a born again, Spirit-filled believer, we have His resurrection power living inside of us. The Holy Spirit empowers us to live like Jesus did. We have His authority to overcome all the schemes and deceptions the enemy of our soul sends us. It is the desire of the Lord that each one of us chooses the Kingdom of God and become Kingdom-minded people, with Kingdom-minded purposes, to establish His dominion in this generation in all we do and say.

God is love. He transforms each and every one of us as we yield to His perfect love. Because I have embraced His transforming love I am compelled to impart the treasures of truth He has revealed to me. Jesus came both to reveal the love of the Father as well as to expose the works of darkness.

The purpose of this book is two fold: to unmask the works of darkness and reveal Biblical prayer strategies that will equip parents to stand in faith against the intents of the enemy in the lives of their children. The enemy's ultimate goal is to destroy our kids' redemption, identity and destiny in Christ. He attempts to captivate and bind their hearts and minds. However, the shed blood of Jesus has provided a way of redemption from the penalty of sin. Early on in my Christian walk, I began to understand that there was a battle in the heavenly realms. That battle was waging war against my heart and mind by keeping me in bondage through old mindsets and patterns of behavior.

It was at this point I realized that despite having given my life to Christ, I still did not experience the fullness of His freedom in my soul.

The Lord began to teach me not only about His work on the cross but also the reality of spiritual warfare. As I began applying these principles and strategies in my personal life I soon saw transformation begin in my heart and mind. Over time, as these strategies were honed in my own life, I began applying them to my growing children as well, especially as they made increasingly more independent decisions and choices. At times their choices led to negative consequences that opened them up to bondage. The recognition and confession of sin is the bases for life in Christ. The drawing of the Holy Spirit leads to a saving knowledge of Jesus Christ their Lord and Savior. This book can be applied to any part of an individual's life, whether it is contending for their salvation or freedom from the effects of sin. I continue to apply these strategies and walk in my dominion here on earth. The blessings are greater measures of His presence, love, joy and peace.

My prayer is that this book will change your life and that your Christian walk will soar to new heights. I pray you will find yourself declaring the word of God with new strength and authority. You are God's chosen individual to declare kingdom principles and see kingdom results. There is no mistake in that. Jesus died to bring us into full restoration in Him, and He rose again to give us power here on earth! You have what it takes to walk in your God-given dominion and release the Kingdom of God in and through your family.

Let His Kingdom invade your home today!

Pastor Cathy Coppola

TESTIMONIES

"Thank you Pastor Cathy for teaching us how to fight back against the devil's schemes. You have made a HUGE impact in my life." Vicky

"We are in a spiritual battle. Jesus came to bring His kingdom to earth and to set the captives free. The biblical strategies to do just that have been taught practically, yet powerfully, by Pastor Cathy Coppola. She lives an astonishing life in Christ and I have been awakened to the degree of spiritual warfare that confronts our children. All of these strategies are essential to enable them to live fully in His love and in the destiny He desires for them." Diana

"The teaching you have given us has been essential for our spiritual growth." Louise

"I cannot thank you enough for your prayers. I am stronger and have more energy and focus since coming to your meetings. Additionally, your teaching is so valuable as it is not easy to recognize his subtle tactics. Thank you, thank you, thank you for your love, obedience and dedication to our Savior!" Judy

"I'm done with doubting myself, more than trusting Jesus' power IN ME!

You are a lovely example spirituality that is meek and powerful! You walk in honor and are a true Ambassador for Jesus! I'm so grateful for you!" Kirsten

I know as you read this book and begin applying the strategies, you too will have a testimony of how God is turning the hearts of the children back to the fathers. ***Malachi 4:6***

Introduction

THE POWER IS WITHIN YOU

This book is about spiritual warfare. It describes how to destroy the works of the enemy and release the power of God here on earth.

Isaiah 14 describes the fall of the angel Lucifer, now called Satan, the devil, the deceiver, the enemy himself.

The Kingdom of God is advancing against the darkness of the enemy. *Matthew 11:12*

Believers in Jesus Christ are the army of God. We are powerful in Him and will not shrink back to any deception of the enemy.

We will fight for our kids using spiritual weapons of warfare, in confidence, and win this battle for their soul.

Regardless of what your situation looks like at

the present moment, the enemy is not as powerful as God.

The enemy wants you to doubt the power of God, but he is a liar and the father of lies. Don't listen to him.

In writing this book, I desire to help parents who have watched their kids make poor choices, leaving them susceptible, falling captive to the voices of this culture.

The enemy's goal is to deceive the hearts and minds of our kids and lead them down a destructive path. He will try to harden their heart and cause them to fall into sin. He wants to steer them way from making a decision to live for Christ.

To every parent who set out to raise their kids to love and honor the Lord but are feeling shamed and discouraged regarding the choices their kids have made, I'm here to tell you that you can be that forerunner that causes Heaven to invade your home and arrest the darkness around it.

Regardless of what has happened, there is still hope for your kids. It is not too late. You have not failed as a parent. The word of God is full of promises to stand on and reclaim those kids even though they may be spiritually far away.

This book will address strategic principles of power and action for you to use starting today.

Before we begin, we must realize that Christian parents have resurrection power living inside of them. That resurrection power is life-giving power. It has power to speak to what is dead and call it back to life. Jesus is our example, and the word of God is our authority.

Jesus not only died to forgive us our sins, but He rose again to give us resurrection power.

He rose from the dead. His Spirit is in every believer who has committed his/her life to Him. His resurrection power is in you!

You are a mighty warrior, and within you is the power to cause change in the lives of your kids. Jesus Christ in you has all power and authority to destroy the plans of the enemy within your family. *Luke 10:19* He lives in the lives of every committed believer. If Jesus is your Lord and Savior, then you have all you need to be an agent of change in the lives of your kids. You have resurrection power. Whatever is dead or dormant in your life and/or in the lives of your kids will soon come to life. It is time to step out of the grave clothes and into His divine power today!

What You Will Receive From This Book

If your kids, regardless of their age, are currently under deception and have fallen into the ways of the world, this book will teach you six strategies of power and action, allowing you to be the agent of change to cause Heaven to pour into their lives and transform them. These strategies work, as they are scriptural. I used them when my family was in turmoil and my kids were taken captive by the devil's deceit. And, I now use these same strategies when I counsel others, and they too have seen great results.

With proven strategies that the Lord personally gave me, this book will help parents be proactive in getting back what belongs to them: the hearts' of their children. In this book, you will find practical, faith-filled steps to stand in the gap and believe in God for your kids, even when they may have stopped believing for themselves.

Through these strategies, this book will teach you how to:

- Rise up in faith and not take what the devil throws your way as the final answer

- Declare war on the devil's plans and overthrow and destroy his schemes against your family

- Release Heaven's blessings in your kids' lives even when they are as far away from the Lord as possible

Regardless of what your kids have fallen into, the power of God, through one faithful vessel on earth, can snatch those kids out of deception and bring them back into their rightful mind.

Have your kids made poor, devastating choices in life?

If you follow these proven strategies that the Lord gave me, you can turn a horrible situation around and cause it to work out for good. God's word has the power to completely change a negative circumstance and overthrow the deception the enemy brought in.

Are they being influenced by the wrong crowd and become completely different from the way they were raised?

You can be the one who wins them back and snatches them from the lies that have ensnared them.

Have your kids fallen into drugs?

The statistics are that nine out of ten people who become addicted to hard core drugs never come out of them alive. I'm here to tell you there is hope in spite of the statistics. Your kids can be that one in ten! Don't let the world define their future. Don't let the statistics declare their destiny. God's word declares their destiny. You need to take His word and learn how to destroy the works of the devil and advance the Kingdom of God.

God wants to use you in their lives. Are you willing to be used by God to snatch your kids out of the devil's trap?

Don't put off reading this book. The time is now. You don't have time to lose. Your kids don't have time to lose. They need you to step up and fight until they choose to fight for themselves.

You can because the power is within you, the power of the resurrection. *Luke 17:21*

The Lies of Satan

I believe the enemy has plagued the minds of many parents, and they have bought into the devil's lies:

- "The situation is too far gone."

- "My kids are older, and I cannot reach their hearts anymore."

- "If I would have known years ago what I know now, I could have helped my kids when they were young, but that time has passed. It's too late now."

These are all lies!

The truth is that today is the day of salvation. *2 Corinthians 6:2* Although we cannot go back and change what was done in the past, we have all power and authority to change the outcome of this day and the days to come. It's never too late to be an effective agent of change.

You have the power to change. Your kids have the power to change. Every person has the power to change, regardless of the behavior he/she may be displaying today. With God all things are possible. *Matthew 19:26*

Satan's War Against Your Kids

Although you may feel like you have laid your life down for your kids, and it seems like it was useless because everything is in shambles right now, it is not. You need to walk by faith rather than walking by what you see. Persistence is the key. Be persistent in your faith. You are tearing down strongholds that have kept your kids in bondage for years. Don't move from your post. You are on assignment.

Many times when kids rebel, it is a cry for love. They've been wounded and don't know how to properly handle their pain. There are many reasons why this occurs, but regardless of why, I believe they are all looking for love. Only the love of God can truly satisfy them and bring them the peace they are seeking, their peace with God. You can be the instrument of love in their lives and help turn things around.

In my own family, the devastation that hit our home almost destroyed us. As deception began filling their hearts, their choices caused them to drift further and further away. The onslaught of the devil was harsh and fierce. But God! He intervened. He taught me how to fight the good fight of faith in the midst of the storm.

He taught me how to rise up with authority and by faith, snatch them out of deception. He taught me how to be strong in the face of physical danger and spiritual attacks. He taught me how to stay in His love even though war waged all around me. He taught me how to wage war against the devil and win.

I give Him all the glory for He is faithful and will be faithful in your situation as well.

We must understand that there is a war against our kids' souls. We were created to love and worship the Lord. When we choose to fill that need apart from God we will find ourselves searching for significance, value and belonging in other ways. The ways of the world will never satisfy nor bring true peace with God. *For all that is in the world – the lust of the flesh, the lust of the eyes, and the pride of life – is not of the Father but is of the world. 1 John 2:16* When our children choose to walk in the flesh, the enemy sees his opportunities and strikes. He sees vulnerability and weakness in us all and does not play fair.

Let's look at what the word of God says about what the devil is doing on earth to come against our kids.

Be sober, be vigilant, because your adversary the devil walks about like a roaring lion, seeking whom he may devour. *1 Peter 5:8*

The enemy, the adversary, studies us. He is studying our kids. He repeatedly speaks lies to our kids' minds, and because they are vulnerable, they buy into the lie. Slowly, they become deceived, devoured by the lies a little at a time.

They begin to believe the lie that they are not loved or accepted so they might as well go along with those enticing them down the wrong path. This is a subtle trap the enemy uses to deceive them and separate them from those who really do love them. *2 Timothy 2:26*

The prince of this world has many well-laid traps that work in conjunction with the works of the flesh. *Galatians 5:19* These traps are schemes the enemy uses once they have chosen to walk in the flesh. As a by-product of these actions, they enter this vortex—this web of deception. Yet, their actions are a cry for help, a cry for love. Not only are they looking to be loved, but also to be known and accepted. We need to know how to go to war against the deception that is enticing them to separate from their family and their faith in Jesus Christ. With that said, sometimes they refuse the truth and want their own way. When they push against us and reject what we have taught them, it hurts, and it can be very frightening. We must remember that each one of us has a free will; therefore, we cannot make anyone do anything they don't want to do. Yet, this does not mean we are powerless. God's word is full of scripture telling us how to break the deception around them and release the truth.

It is also possible that we may be suffering negative consequences from someone else's decisions. Yet, our outcome in life is not about what happens to us, but with what we do with what happens to us. That determines our future. We must understand we do not fight against flesh and blood, but against a spiritual war waged against us.

For we do not wrestle against flesh and blood, but against principalities, against powers, against the rulers of the darkness of this age, against spiritual hosts of wickedness in the heavenly places. Ephesians 6:12

There is a spiritual battle for the lives of our kids. The devil does not play fair. He wants to deceive the hearts of your loved ones and plague their minds with his schemes. Our fight is not a fight against our kids. Our fight is against the enemy who has taken captive the minds and hearts of our kids and caused them to act in destructive ways.

We must learn to fight biblically and not budge when the enemy comes against our homes. Remember, this battle is against the enemy of our souls. He is behind all of this and is waging war against you and your kids. Learn to recognize the real enemy, the devil, and declare war on his plan against you and your family.

Change the Spiritual Realm

There are spiritual laws we can activate to cause change in the spiritual realm before we see it in the natural realm. Every strategy I lay out in this book is a spiritual strategy.

As you begin to walk in these strategies and do it everyday, before long you will see the results in the lives of your kids as the Kingdom of Heaven begins invading earth!

Let's begin taking back your kids from the trap of the devil and setting them on the right path for their destiny. Let's learn how to be proactive and declare war on the plan of the enemy and tell him to get his hands off our kids!

Are you ready to jump in? Your loved ones need you to learn these strategies. They will thank you for it someday.

Now to Him who is able to do exceedingly abundantly above all that we ask or think, according to the power that works in us, to Him be glory in the church by Christ Jesus to all generations, forever and ever. Amen. **Ephesians 3:20 & 22**

If you have raised your kids to love and honor the Lord, but they have been enticed by the world and are making poor choices, get ready to step in to God's divine strategies and see the power of God start to transform their lives.

Devil!

GET YOUR HANDS OFF!

6 STRATEGIES TO SNATCH YOUR KIDS OUT OF DECEPTION

Chapter One

STRATEGY ONE: THE POWER OF YOUR DECREE

There is so much power in your spoken words. Are you building up or tearing down? Speaking life or speaking death? Creating life or destroying it? Your words carry power to either bless or curse. When you speak something and do not doubt in your heart, the Bible says in Mark 11:23–25 you will have what you say. It will be done for you as long as it is in accordance with God's will.

Your words produce results. It is your responsibility to align your words with Heaven and witness the power of God in action in the lives of your kids. It is possible! Not only are your words powerful, they can change the very atmosphere you live in. The power of your decree is in your mouth! It is spoken out loud regardless if your kids are present or not. Your words have the power to change their very lives.

When you align your words with God's word, you have the highest authority backing up what you say. God's word will not return to you void.

So shall My word be that goes forth from My mouth. It shall not return to Me void. But is shall accomplish what I please and it shall prosper in the thing for which I sent it. Isaiah 55:11

It is a promise.

Regardless of the spiritual state your kids are in, as you rise up in faith and declare God's truth for their lives, Heaven backs you up!

This is how it works. When you speak God's word about your children out loud, the angels of God go to work to bring it to pass.

Bless the Lord, you His angels. Who excel in strength, who do His word, heeding the voice of His word. Psalm 103:20

The angels of God heed the voice of God's word and do it—they bring it to pass! Are you speaking the word of God in your circumstances, therefore, causing the angels of God to go to work? This is your right as a son or daughter of the living God.

The Lord is watching over His word to perform it. **Jeremiah 1:12**

He is waiting for you to speak forth His word, in faith, so He can bring it to pass.

I am the Lord who carries out the words of His servants and fulfills the predictions of His messengers. **Isaiah 44:26**

What I speak, God will carry out!

There is more power in the words you speak than you may realize. The Bible tells us we have the power to produce life or death just by speaking! Ask yourself, what are you speaking? What are you releasing out of your mouth: life or death?

The Difference Between Words of Life and words of Death

- Words of life are words that will help bring others into their destiny. Words that will build them up and set them free from bondage.

- Words of death are words that will produce any kind of death in others' lives, tearing them down leading them to destruction. These are words that will keep them stuck in a far less than victorious life.

Your words are more powerful than you realize.

***Death and life are in the power of the tongue, and those who love it will eat its fruit.* Proverbs 18:21**

What fruit is being produced in the lives of your kids? If there is bad fruit, there is a bad root. You can speak the word of God, which is the seed, and it will be planted in the ground of their hearts. Your seed can produce good fruit for them!

This principle works the same both in the natural realm and the spiritual realm. In the natural realm, if you plant a seed and it grows into a tree but it produces bad fruit, you can be sure that at some point in time the root was negatively affected, and, therefore, the fruit is now defective.

The same is true in your life. When you plant negative words or allow others to plant negative words in the lives of your kids, and they take root, they will produce negative fruit. Negative agreements partner with the devil, and he heaps upon their lives a heavy weight of deception. You must deal with the root in order to change the behavior so the fruit produced will be good.

As you plant God's word in your kid's lives, regardless of their age, that word will eventually take root. It will produce Heaven's fruit, which is that good and pleasant return. Your words can and will make a change in the lives of your kids when your words align with the will of God.

A Secret the Devil Does Not Want You to Know About

The enemy has secrets he uses against you, and he does not want you to find out about them.

When you release words of life with your mouth, you are releasing arrows laced with venom into the enemy's camp. Think about that image for a second: an arrow laced with poison shot right into the enemy's camp, destroying the ambushes before they destroy your kids.

Your words are like those arrows. What words are you speaking? What are you decreeing? The Lord showed me years ago to never align my words with the devil.

Are you giving Satan an advantage in their lives?

When you give voice to their negative state of mind, you are reinforcing the devil's will by speaking the obvious.

When you speak words of life to someone, you are speaking death to the enemy!

This is the secret the enemy does not want you to know about.

Did you catch that?

When you speak life-giving words—words that build up, words that bring hope, and words full of faith—you are destroying the enemy's trap that he laid out for the lives of your loved ones.

This is the secret the enemy does not want you to know about and certainly does not what you to understand or take to heart.

When you speak negative words—words that bring shame, judgments, and instill fear and doubt—you are partnering with the devil and reinforcing his will.

The Devil Is Waiting on Your Mouth

The devil is waiting on your mouth to agree with his plan for your kids. It may be a fact that your kids are bound in addiction. But that is the enemy's will for their lives.

It may be a fact that they have rebelled, and they are hanging out with the wrong crowd. But that is the enemy's well laid out strategy to entrap them.

It may be a fact that they have strayed from their faith, don't go to church, and you don't see good fruit in their lives. But that is the result of the enemy's lie in their lives.

Never agree with the devil's plan for your family by verbalizing it and saying it as truth. Be wise in the words you speak.

Don't allow yourself to speak words like:

- "Well my son or daughter is a drug addict and will probably always be one." That is a spoken curse. That curse needs to be broken. It needs to be canceled.

- "Well my daughter is probably going to get pregnant out of wedlock if she keeps going in this direction." You are speaking word curses over your kids.

- "I'd be surprised if my kids finish school. They'll probably drop out or be kicked out." This is a word curse. Never agree with the devil's plans for your family's life by verbalizing it.

More Words of Death

- My kids are so rebellious.

- They will only learn the hard way.

- They are just like their father/mother.

- My kids will never amount to anything.

- They will never learn.

- They will always be in trouble.

- If they don't stop what they are doing, they are going to kill themselves.

Can you see that even if there is truth to those statements, by aligning yourself with them, you are helping those negative situations come to pass? The word of God tells us you will have what you say; therefore, you need to be careful and not careless in what you speak. When a person speaks something and begins to believe what he/she says, it will begin to take root.

You shall have what you say. Mark 11:23

Death and life are in the power of the tongue, and those who love it will eat its fruit. Proverbs 18:21

Your words spoken over your kids' lives have a lot of power to help or hinder their future.

Speak life over your kids and produce life even when they have made bad decisions, and they find themselves in a terrible mess.

If you speak what's obvious to your natural eye, you may be producing death in their lives.

I am not saying to deny there is a problem. I am saying not to give it more weight than what God's word says over them. Our kids have free will. Their poor choices may give them lasting negative results. But we, as parents, can be used by God to put the odds in their favor and be a life-giver in their lives.

The Devil Is A Liar

There is nothing good in him. His only agenda is to *"steal, kill, and destroy."* **John 10:10** He tries to steal the hearts of your kids, and then he tries to attack your heart with fear that they will never return. He is a liar. Don't give him any satisfaction with any agreement in your heart. Remember who he is: a fallen angel that has an eternal destiny of damnation. **Luke 10:18**

Your words have the power to destroy the enemy's plan. There is power in your spoken word regardless of what you see happening all around you. Don't live by what you see, but by every word that comes from the mouth of God. **Matthew 4:4**

You are their parent. You are the authoritative figure in their life. Your words carry weight; that weight is either going to be good weight or bad weight. It will either produce a blessing or a curse in their life. **James 3:10**

Your kids need you to rise up in faith and speak God's truth, not the negative circumstances you may be seeing in their lives.

Your kids need you to speak out the living words of God into the atmosphere and cause a supernatural change to affect their lives. *Job 22:28* You have the power and authority to do this.

Your kids need you to be their greatest cheerleader, their advocate, and the one who has never stopped believing in them. Your kids need you to stand strong, to believe, and to speak the truth, which is based on the word of God and not based on their actions. Regardless of their actions today, they need your faith.

The devil has deceived them. Therefore, their actions follow suit. They are carrying out what they believe. But God has given you insight, His heavenly wisdom. He has given you power. He has given you authority to snatch your kids out of the devil's grip by speaking forth the truth in spite of what you see them doing; in spite of what you hear them saying; in spite of what may be all around you. Your decree is one of the most powerful things you have.

If your decree is negative, it will partner with the enemy and continue to destroy their lives.

Regardless of the circumstances, regardless of where they are going or how they are currently living, your weapons of warfare have never changed. They remain the same. They are intact, and they are very effective. They are mighty in God!

For the weapons of our warfare are not carnal but mighty in God for pulling down strongholds, casting down arguments and every high thing that exalts itself against the knowledge of God, bringing every thought into captivity to the obedience of Christ, and being ready to punish all disobedience when your obedience is fulfilled. 2 Corinthians 10:4–6

Your words have the power to pull down strongholds that have been built up for years! Your words have power to cast down anything that stands contrary to the word of God in their lives! How powerful is that? Why do we take so long to understand this powerful gift before using it? Because the enemy tries to deceive us as parents. He doesn't want you to understand how simple but how true and effective your words are.

The Power of Two

It only takes two to agree on earth.

Again I say to you that if two of you agree on earth concerning anything that they ask, it will be done for them by My Father in heaven. **Matthew 18:19**

There is power in agreeing with someone in accordance with the will of God in an effort to bring that request to come to pass.

Yet, this same principle can be used in agreeing with what the enemy desires for your life.

What about when you agree with the enemy, and believe his lies about your kids?

What about when you voice with your mouth that they will never come out of the mental state they are in. What about when you voice with your mouth that they will always be troublemakers, always suffer from this disease, never make enough money, always struggle with drugs or alcohol.

Whom are you agreeing with?

When you speak these types of statements, you are not agreeing with God's will, but the enemy's will for your kids.

The Enemy Has a Will for Your Life

Believers are not immune to falling for the enemy's will in their lives.

Paul writes to the church, *That they may come to their senses and escape the snare of the devil, having been taken captive to do his will*. *2 Timothy 2:26*

The devil tries to ensnare us and take us captive to do his will!

The devil is waiting on you, the parental authority figure, to operate in fear and partner with his plan. Your agreement with him will ensnare your kids.

Don't agree with hell regarding your kids' lives however real it may seem. Only God is true. The word states *let God be true and every man a liar*. *Romans 3:4*

How Does the Word of God Affect the Negative Powers Influencing our Kids' Lives?

When your decree is based on the word of God, the devil hears you, and he flees. *James 4:7* He cannot stand the decree of the Lord. He knows the power that is in the living word of God. Jesus is the living word. When the devil came to tempt Jesus in Matthew chapter 4, Jesus responded with the word of God. He said, "It is written." After the devil tempted Jesus three times, he left Him until a more opportune time. Jesus is our example. We are to use the word of God against the plans of the enemy and be persistent.

If the devil tried to come against Jesus to tempt him into questioning God's word and promises who are we to think he won't come against us to make us doubt God's word? This plan of his is not a new plan. There is nothing new under the sun. *Ecclesiastes 1:9* He will tell you it is too late for your kids. He will tell you they are so far gone they will never return to the Lord. He will make it seem very true in an attempt to cause you to give up and speak whatever you see and feel. He wants to tell you the situation is so bad you might as well stop praying for them.

God's word is a weapon to use against the onslaughts of the enemy. Never forget this powerful truth, regardless of what your circumstances are dictating at the moment. The word of God is the sword of the Spirit, which is a powerful weapon.

And take the helmet of salvation, and the sword of the Spirit, which is the word of God; praying always with all prayer and supplication in the Spirit,

***being watchful to this end with all
perseverance and supplication for all
the saints.*** *Ephesians 6:17 & 18*

God's spoken word has the power to snatch
those you love from a pit of destruction and
open their eyes to the truth. Once the eyes of
their hearts are opened, they will be able to
make better choices for their lives.

Paul prayed that those he was ministering to
would have wisdom and revelation and that the
eyes of their understanding would be
enlightened.

***That the God of our Lord Jesus Christ,
the Father of glory, may give to you the
spirit of wisdom and revelation in the
knowledge of Him, the eyes of your
understanding being enlightened; that
you may know what is the hope of His
calling, what are the riches of the glory
of His inheritance in the saints, and
what is the exceeding greatness of His
power toward us who believe,
according to the working of His mighty
power which He worked in Christ when
He raised Him from the dead and seated
Him at His right hand in the heavenly
places, far above all principality and***

power and might and dominion, and every name that is named, not only in this age but also in that which is to come. And He put all things under His feet and gave Him to be head over all things to the church, which is His body, the fullness of Him who fills all in all.
Ephesians 1:17–23

There is an exceedingly great power available for those who believe in the resurrected Christ. He rose triumphantly over the grave. All principalities, power, might and dominion are under His authority. Therefore, if you are in Christ, all things are under your feet, for you are seated with Him in the heavenly places.
Ephesians 2:6

Therefore, we have power over every negative influence working against our kids with the words we decree.

In spite of what they say or do, if it does not line up with God's word, step in and be the one God uses.

Decree the truth. God's word is truth over their lives.

You shall decree a thing and it shall be established for you, so light will shine on your ways. Job 22:28

Speak it into Existence and Raise What is Dead to Life

In Christ, we carry His DNA. We are created in His image. His Spirit lives inside of us. Therefore, we are to be imitators of Christ. What He did, we should do.

God gives life to the dead and calls those things, which do not exist as though they did. Romans 4:17

In what area of your kids' lives is there spiritual death? Has hope been lost? Where have they strayed into the trap of this world?

You can be the one who speaks to the darkness and awakens life! Speak life into your kids' lives with full authority, knowing if Jesus did it, so can you! *Ephesians 5:1*

You can speak to what is dead or seems dead and call it back to life. For example if the situation seems hopeless, don't agree with what you see in the natural. Call what is dead back to life in prayer.

"In the name of Jesus, I speak life to every hopeless place in my kids' life. I declare hope to arise again." *Isaiah 60:1*

"In the name of Jesus, I command the spiritual blinders to fall off their eyes and the eyes of their understanding to be opened." *Ephesians 1:18*

"In the name of Jesus, I call forth every dormant gift the Lord has given them and declare they walk in their heavenly gifting without compromise." *Romans 4:17*

"In the name of Jesus, I command every place of deception to be broken off their life and the truth of Christ to arise within them." *Mark 16:17*

Weighty Words

Words carry weight. God created the world with them. His word is creative power. His word declares that we are to be imitators of Christ.

That means you should speak as He speaks and believe that when you speak, change is happening even if for a while you don't see it with your natural eyes.

If your decree is in partnership with the word of God, it will produce abundance because your words carry weight.

> In Genesis we read that God spoke, **"Let there be light."** And there was light. ***Genesis 1:3***

> In the Gospels we read that Jesus spoke to the fig tree and cursed it, and it shriveled up from the root. ***Mark 11:20***

> Jesus spoke to the wind and waves and said, **"Be still,"** and the waves became still. ***Mark 4:39***

> He spoke to a man dead four days, and said, **"Lazarus, come forth."** And he came forth. ***John 11:43***

> He spoke life, and life was produced. He created from nothing because He is God Almighty. ***John 1:4 & 5***

Thus, we can create from what God has given us. He left us His word and expects us to use that word as a weapon to bring about the change we need. He gave us His resurrection power and expects us to use it to produce life even out of what seems dead. He is the author of life, and He is our source!

He gave us the substance in words to cause life or death just by what we speak! That is powerful.

Because Christ lives within us, we have the same potential. When you see your kids in the place of destruction, call them out of that destruction by the power of your decree. When you see your kids deceived and in a rebellious state of mind, begin using the word of God and cause your words to line up with Heaven in their life. The word will never return void. Make it your decree.

Your words have potential to cause a lot of change. Are you using them to create or destroy the ones you love the most? Line up your words with the word of God. In order to do this, you must know what His word says. Use the scriptures. His word is Holy, powerful, effective, and life giving.

Ask the Holy Spirit to lead you. Personalize them and begin declaring them out loud daily. This is called standing on the promises of God. This is your call to action; really believe God's word as you speak it out loud, knowing it will cause change because His word is alive.

I did this consistently before I began seeing the change in my kids. Even if you do not see immediate results, don't give up.

Your words are powerful and cause significant change. Use them to create, not destroy the ones you love the most.

Powerful Decrees to Make

- *All my children will be taught of the Lord and great will be their peace. Isaiah 54:13*

- *I will contend with him who contends with you, and your children I will save. Isaiah 49:25*

- *My Spirit who is upon you, and My words which I have put in your mouth, shall not depart from your mouth, nor from the mouth of your children, nor from the mouth of your children's children. Isaiah 59:21*

- *The posterity of the righteous shall be delivered. Proverbs 11:21*

- *As for me and my house, we shall serve the Lord.* **Joshua 24:15**

- **My kids are God fearing.**

- **They have a heart for God.**

- **They walk in integrity.**

- **They are honest and law abiding people.**

- **They put a high value on family.**

- **They value life as the most precious gift given to them.**

- **My kids walk with God.**

There cannot be any doubt when you declare these truths. God's word never lies. Therefore, you must speak strong, powerful, effective decrees aligned with the word of God. Your decrees will then cause the circumstances to come into alignment with His word.

Time to Take Action

This strategy has been tried and tested, and it works! It works whether you realize it or not. It works whether you are intentionally using this strategy or not. Use this principle as a positive weapon against all the darkness coming against your family, knowing that the Lord is waiting on your words to bring them to pass.

Remember, you carry weight in the realms of the spirit. Watch your words and be intentional about what you speak.

Since the battle in the heavenly realm is real and it is a war for your kids' souls, remember to align your words with Heaven and see the power of God to rescue your family.

Keep saying the same thing. God's word is true.

God is not a man, that He should lie, nor a son of man, that He should change His mind. Does He speak and not act, or promise and not fulfill? Numbers 23:19

When God speaks, He acts; when He promises, He fulfills. The Bible is His heart expressed in words. It is our promise to hold on to and agree with.

Therefore, when we speak in accordance with the word of God, we know all of Heaven is backing up our decrees. Speak His word. It is a powerful weapon to cause positive change.

Declare the promises of God out loud daily until you see the change you desire.

Don't miss a day, even if you don't see change or you see things getting worse.

Don't allow negative setbacks to stop you from using this powerful, proven strategy.

Regardless of how long your situation lasts, never give up. God never gives up on you. You need to align your words with God's word.

You need to make the right decrees in the midst of the war zone, in the midst of the problem.

When you see a critical situation, you need to rise up within and state your decree with power. There is a forerunner in every family; a forerunner that carries authority. Since you are reading this book, chances are you are the forerunner in your family. God has given you His delegated authority to walk right into the enemy's camp and snatch what rightfully belongs to you.

So let your agreement be with the Kingdom of Heaven and allow the power of God to shift the atmosphere for you as you partner with the King of Kings and the Lord of Lords who is mighty to save!

In Review

- Your words are powerful carriers of change in your kids' lives. Align your words with God's word and watch Heaven invade your circumstances.

- It's your job to speak, and God's job to make it come to pass.

- Don't agree with the enemy. Speak words that produce life not death, words that build up not destroy.

- Words of life destroy the plan of the enemy.

- Call those things that do not exist as though they did, just as Jesus did.

- Be intentional about making your decree and continue with your decree until it comes to pass.

In the next chapter, we are going to talk about our delegated authority and how we can use it to rightfully claim what should have never been stolen: the hearts of our kids.

Chapter Two

STRATEGY TWO: THE POWER OF YOUR AUTHORITY

We all have obstacles and mountains in our lives that come against us, situations that make moving forward difficult. But, we have the authority in Christ to move the mountains blocking our family from going forward. Using our authority, we can destroy the devil's devices and bring forth the God-given destiny in our family's life when we learn to use it according to God's principles.

Your second strategy is the power of authority.

Your authority is your right to do something. You have a God-given right to declare war on the schemes of the enemy on behalf of your children.

In *1 Peter 5:8* the Bible tells us that "**the devil prowls around like a roaring lion seeking someone to devour. Regardless** of this fact, Jesus gave us authority over the power of the devil."

Behold, I give you the authority to trample on serpents and scorpions, and over all the power of the enemy, nothing shall by any means hurt you.
Luke 10:19

Nothing shall by any means hurt you. Nothing means nothing!

Jesus did not give you some authority—He gave you all authority.

His Authority Was Not Just For the Disciples

It is for you!

In *Luke 9:1* Jesus gave power and authority to his twelve disciples to rid people of demons and to cure diseases.

Then in *Luke 10:1* Jesus appointed seventy others and sent them out two by two and gave them power and authority. Verse 19 of Luke 10 states that they have power and authority over all the power of the enemy.

Jesus then spoke the Great Commission for all who would believe in Him.

In *Mark 16:17* He said, **"these signs shall follow those who believe; In My name they will cast out demons; they will speak with new tongues; they will take up serpents; and if they drink anything deadly, it will by no means hurt them; they will lay hands on the sick, and they will recover."**

You have authority to cast out any demonic power operating against you and your kids! Every believer has authority over the works of the devil. You must learn how to use your weapon of authority.

If you don't take authority over the works of darkness in the lives of your kids, the demonic influence will grow, and your kids will become further and further deceived and distant. Whatever sin you tolerate in life will steal from you. Whatever sin you ignore will increase.

Whatever you capture, you conquer. It's time to rise up in authority and kick out those spirits that don't belong in your home.

Kick out every spirit of rebellion, idolatry, pride, stubbornness, illicit drugs, promiscuity, compromise, apathy and any other spirits you believe are in operation.

You have power and authority in the name of Jesus to bind up and cast out demon forces that have plagued your kids' lives.

How to Use Your Authority

Assuredly, I say to you, whatever you bind on earth will be bound in heaven, and whatever you loose on earth will be loosed in heaven. Matthew 18:18

You have authority to bind the spirits that are trying to ruin your kids' lives.

When you bind the enemy's work, you are tying it up as with shackles, therefore, stopping all its activity.

Binding and loosening is a biblical concept. Use your authority and bind the spirit that is working against your kids. Bind it by issuing a verbal command for it to be bound in the name of Jesus. **"Devil, I take authority over your work. I bind every spirit of rebellion operating in the lives of my kids in the name of Jesus."**

Command the devil to stop harassing and preventing them from receiving God's blessings in their lives.

"I command every spirit harassing my kids to stop now in Jesus' name. Lord, loose Your favor and Your blessings over their lives."

Step into your God-given authority and rise up in power. Charge against the wicked plans of the enemy. Do not let him defeat you or your loved ones. It is time to fight.

Put Your Armor On: You're In A Battle

Mighty men and women of God, you are in a battle for the lives of your children. Learn to put on the armor daily, for the unseen realm is more real than the visible realm.

No solider would go to battle without his armor and his weapons. So why do we enter unprepared? Just because the battle is an unseen one does not make it any less significant. As a matter of fact, it is so significant that going without your armor may have grave consequences for you and those you love.

Learn to fight right. Though the battle belongs to the Lord, He expects you to rise up in the battle and use your authority. If you did not have any part in this battle, you would have no need for the armor of God.

We know in *Ephesians 6:10–18*, we are commanded to put on the whole armor of God. Part of that armor is the sword of the Spirit, the word of God, which is what we are told to fight with. We use His word and declare it out loud, which shakes the Heavens and brings destruction upon the enemy's camp. The rest of the armor is for your protection.

> The breastplate of righteousness covers your heart and emotions.

> The helmet of salvation is to remind you to keep your mind set on God's word.

> The belt of truth is the word of God and what holds everything together.

> The gospel shoes of peace remind you to walk in the peace of God, knowing you already are victorious through Christ.

> The shield of faith is to block every attack.

The enemy will try to cause you to forget to daily put on the armor of God. He wants you to feel defeated and hopeless because of the damage that has already been done in your family. Mighty warriors, don't take his bait. It is satanic bait meant to instill fear in you to give up the fight. The devil has been defeated on the cross. Jesus already won and rose victoriously over sin, death, and the devil when He shed His blood. *Anything the enemy is doing in your kids' life is because of a partnership he found with sin.* Yet, you still have the authority to rise above his schemes.

It's time to look with your spiritual eyes and see as the Lord sees. Ask Him to increase your discernment, which is a gift that comes from Him. You need greater levels of discernment to know what spirit is in operation against you or your kids. You need to comprehend where you stand in this spiritual battle. As a believer, you are positioned with Christ.

You are seated in heavenly places at the right hand with Jesus. Ephesians 2:6

You have an aerial view. When you see from Heaven's point of view, you can see the struggle your kids are in, and you will know how to fight. They are fighting a spirit they cannot see. This spirit has entangled your kids, and they do not know how to break free. You must rise up with spiritual eyes, bind the devil, and in the name of Jesus, command him to leave your kids now. Your kids need you to step in and help them fight this battle. You cannot win a spiritual battle without using spiritual weapons—God's word and His authority. You are not defeated. Your family is not destroyed even if it looks like they are. With Christ, there is always hope.

Dominion Authority in the Midst of the War

It's time to take dominion. It's time to pray Kingdom prayers that shake the Heavens and destroy the darkness in your family. It's time to rise up in the middle of the war and take back your kids. The enemy will not let go without a fight. But if you keep your eyes on Jesus and stand in authority with the strategies I am giving you, your kids will come out of captivity. You will reclaim what is rightfully yours. Don't allow the devil to take advantage of your kids or carry them away deceived.

When you feel your kids are under attack, pray this prayer out loud.

Dominion Prayer:

"I come in the name of Jesus Christ. Devil, you can't have my kids. I use my God-given authority and set an ambush to your plans. I destroy every wicked agent of deception and every agent of rebellion and idolatry, which you have

sent, against my family. I bind you devil, and I command you to leave my family now.

I release the fire of God to utterly destroy you and all your demon spirits. The finger of God drives you out now. Go to the arid places and never return, in the name of Jesus."

Warrior, you must learn to war against the devil for he is warring against you. *For the Kingdom of heaven suffers violence and the violent take it by force. Matthew 11:12*

Take back what belongs to you. Stop looking at how hopeless the situation appears and start looking at how big God is. Nothing is impossible for those who believe.

The enemy does not want you to get a revelation of this, for he knows his wicked plan against your family will then be destroyed. He knows you will rise up and defeat him because Jesus already defeated him at the cross. Therefore, when you rise up in authority and use the word of God, the devil is trembling in his boots. Jesus is the word of God. Jesus already defeated him. The devil is harassing you and your family because he thought he could get away with it. But since knowledge is power, you have what it takes to defeat him in the name of Jesus and by the power of the Holy Spirit.

Your kids feel the oppression the enemy brings, and they do not know how to deal with it. They begin to feel like it is their entire fault. They begin to come into agreement with the lies the enemy brings upon them, causing them to lose hope. They begin to feel stuck in this vortex with no way of escape.

You need to have wisdom to speak truth into their lives. You need to see the trap that has been set up for them, and on one hand, take authority over the works of the devil, but on another hand, learn how to affirm whom they are. God uses you to affirm their value and their worth as human beings. When they feel beat up by life and so hurt by others, you will need to discern how to speak to your kids so that you can change their negative mindset and help them to believe in whom they really are.

In Review

- Jesus gave you His authority.

- Use your authority to bind up the spirits that are trying to ruin your kids' lives.

- Put on the armor daily and don't fall prey to the enemy's bait.

- Daily pray the Dominion prayer. Soon you will begin seeing change in your kids' lives.

In the next chapter, we will discuss how to break the lies from their thinking so they can begin partnering with the truth and turn their lives around. What you say to them matters. What you don't say to them matters just as much. Who are you partnering with? Are you ready to break off those lies and negative mindsets and bring down the blessings of God for your kids? We will discuss this strategy in the next chapter.

Chapter Three

STRATEGY THREE: THE POWER OF YOUR AFFIRMATION

Hope deferred makes a heart sick. Sometimes when hope is waning and the only thing evident is the harsh consequences and negative circumstances, it is easy to give up and give in to defeat. When kids feel there is no way back, they begin to believe the lies that their life is hopeless and they feel like giving up.

Your kids need you more than you realize. They have been beaten down with the consequences of their bad choices. They already know they have messed up. They already know they are in a bad place. The devil has been harassing them, and they cannot see the way out. You have the power to be a life giver to them by believing who they are in Christ. You have the power to approve and validate who they are without approving of their wrong actions. Affirm who they are in Christ. Unlike the power of your decree, which is spoken without your kids present, the power of your affirmation is spoken in their presence. Your words carry weight and they bring life and hope. The word of God states:

Hope deferred makes a heart sick, but a longing fulfilled is a tree of life. Proverbs 13:12

Now hope does not disappoint because the love of God has been poured out in our hearts by the Holy Spirit who was given to us. Romans 5:5

Even though hope deferred makes a heart sick, God's love poured in their hearts will cause them to shine and come out of hopelessness. We can be the instruments God uses to speak hope and encouragement to them.

Be Their Greatest Cheerleaders

Your kids know they are not where they should be. They feel the weight of their choices. Since they may not see a way out of their mess or they may have given up hope, you can act as a life-giver to them and affirm whom God made them to be.

They need to hear you speak life over them. They need to know that although the rest of the world may have given up on them, you will never give up on them and neither will God. They need you to tell them their worth and their identity in Christ, for they have lost their way.

I remember when I spoke these affirmations in my kids. At that time they did not believe them, but I kept on telling them. I could see in their eyes they didn't have faith in the truth of these words, but they were hanging on to my faith. I knew that I needed to be confident for the both of us. I knew what God's word said. My faith was in His word.

He has never failed me. He will never fail you. Speak affirming words to your kids even when they act as far from them as possible. Their spirit will hear and receive your affirmations. Eventually, they will hear it enough and began to believe it. Once they believe in what you have been saying, it will become part of who they are. In time, they will change their actions to match this belief. So keep affirming them even if they don't appear to be receiving it. Below are some life giving affirmations to speak over them. Allow the Holy Spirit to direct you in specific life-giving affirmations that fit the needs of your kids and speak life to them.

Life-giving Affirmations

- You are more than a conqueror.

- You will fulfill your destiny.

- You have a great destiny and are successful in everything you put your hand to.

- God has given you a great mind, and you use it to bring forth good.

- You have a heart of compassion for people.

- You have a gift to look beyond people's exterior hard shell and see the pain in an individual's life.

- God has given you wisdom and a great mind.

- You will accomplish great things.

- You will go far in life.

- You will make a great husband, wife, teacher, nurse, doctor, engineer, artist, dancer, entrepreneur . . . .

Let Hope Arise

The principle of an affirmation is no different than what the Bible says in *Romans 4:17*, **God, who gives life to the dead and calls those things that do not exist as though they did.**

Did you get that? God looks at something dead and calls it back to life. He calls things that are not here as though they were. He speaks hope to a hopeless situation. He speaks life to a lifeless situation. He has spiritual eyes to see. You, too, need to see with your spiritual eyes.

All through out the word of God this principle is practiced. We can read from Genesis to Revelation examples of God telling us who we are in Christ. He calls us His own beloved sons and daughters. He refers to us as more than conquerors and tells us greater things we shall do in Him. He speaks to us as the apple of His eye and mighty warriors in the faith. We are His ambassadors, His mouthpiece, and His delegated authority here on earth. We are His craftsmanship created to fulfill His eternal purposes. Nothing will stop His will from coming into fruition in our lives unless we let it. We carry His DNA. His very life running in our veins to accomplish His divine will. The principle of affirmation is found throughout the pages of scripture, and acts as a model to use in our lives and the lives of our kids.

Look into the dark, empty places of their lives and call out their destiny. What area looks dead? Speak life to it. Don't be moved by what you see. Be moved by what God says. Call them out of darkness by affirming them in their God-given qualities.

Believe in them, even when they have given up on themselves.

Tell them you believe in them, that the God who lives in them will give them strength and new hope to accomplish great things.

What's Really Going On

When kids are stuck in bad habits with bad friends, you may think that they are not interested in changing, but in reality, they are just afraid to fail. It seems easier for them to remain in their negative circumstances surrounded by people who do the same things, then to rise up and out of the mess their choices led them to.

They need you to affirm them. They need to hear you tell them who they really are. They need to know you believe in them. They need your love more than ever.

When we fall into the pattern of only looking at the grave sin in their lives, the enemy has us again, and we begin loosing the battle to win them back.

Keep your eyes on Jesus, the author and perfector of your faith, knowing that your faith will move mountains. Those mountains in your family's life are your opportunity to see God move in a powerful way. Love your kids back to life. Love is the most powerful thing we have. Love always wins.

In Review

Be their greatest cheerleaders. Believe in them even when they don't believe in themselves.

Use your words to affirm who they are not necessarily what they are doing.

Speak life to any dead areas in their lives and call them back to life.

What happens when you have done all these things, and yet you see no change at all? What happens when you know their choices are very destructive and their hearts are hardened to the sin in their life? This next strategy is very powerful in snatching them out from deception. In the next chapter, we will discuss the strategy that was a major turning point in my family's life as it prevented those I love from destroying their life.

Chapter Four

STRATEGY FOUR: THE POWER OF STANDING IN THE GAP

Standing in the gap means doing something for someone that they cannot or will not do for themselves at this point in time. Standing in the gap means doing what is required so the condition is fulfilled. Using the strategy of standing in the gap is vital for your children's well-being.

When your kids are in sin, there is a requirement that needs to be met. Repentance and forgiveness needs to take place, or the consequences will be great.

Sometimes, even with repentance and forgiveness, the consequences are still great, but unconfessed and unrepented sin will lead to far greater consequences.

The enemy thrives on unconfessed and unrepented sin. Although everyone is responsible for their own sin, there is a time and place where they are not consciously aware of their sin because of the demonic deception and a hardened heart.

Yet, a requirement of forgiveness must be made or grave consequences will be sure to fall. Unconfessed and unrepented sin gives the devil a legal right in your children's lives. It is an open door to the demonic.

The legal rights the enemy has over their lives because of their sin will overtake them in destruction. The war for their soul is on.

Life is like a game of chess: it becomes move, counter-move, move, counter-move. Every move by them releases either the demonic realm or the realm of God. If the demonic realm is released over them, our God-given mandate to stand in the gap must be carried out or the demonic strategy against their life will overtake them.

There is something you can do. One person needs to see with heaven's eyes and have the spiritual wisdom to rise above it all, one person with insight and revelation.

Prolonged Sin Brings Demonic Deception

When sin is not dealt with properly, it brings a demonic deception, and then the person becomes a prisoner in his or her own mind. A film covers their eyes, and their heart becomes hardened to God's truth.

They are bound in iniquity and become a prisoner of war. They need you to see their true spiritual condition and begin removing the iron bars of deception and break the legal rights the enemy has over them.

Sin brings deception, and deception, ultimately, brings death.

When they are deceived, they are not in their right mind and they need you to stand in the gap and repent for their wrongs until the day comes that they will confess and repent for their own sin.

But if you have bitter envy and self-seeking in your hearts, do not boast and lie against the truth. This wisdom does not descend from above but is earthly, sensual, and demonic. For where envy and self-seeking exist, confusion and every evil thing are there. *James 3:14–16*

Prolonged sin brings deception that is not to be taken lightly. It brings in every evil thing. Demonic deception and oppression are sure to follow.

As believing parents who understand the importance of confessing sin, rise up and allow your voice to be heard for the lives of your kids who have been plagued by sin's deceitfulness.

Great Men of Faith Who Stood in the Gap for Others

There are many examples in the Bible where someone stood on behalf of another and asked the Lord to forgive that person and repented on his/her behalf. Here are just a few examples.

- Daniel stood in the gap and repented for Israel's sin. Babylon was an idolatrous nation who worshipped and praised their god, Baal. Daniel, a man of God, was kidnapped and brought to live in a pagan culture. However, he stood strong in the midst of a godless society and prayed for the captive Israelites. He asked the Lord to forgive them of their wicked sin of idolatry. Even though Daniel did not participate in the idolatrous acts, he still prayed and included himself when he asked the Lord to forgive them. Daniel was a godly man, yet he stood in humility and God heard his prayer for the nation. Daniel was used by God to save his people from the enemy's grip. *Daniel 10*

- Ezra, the priest, stood and prayed for the Lord to forgive Israel when they had fallen in unbelief, had been taken captive, and their city was destroyed. Ezra was used by God to bring restoration to the people of Israel by rebuilding the temple. *Ezra 9*

- Abraham prayed to the Lord and asked if He would spare the city of Sodom and Gomorrah if there were ten righteous people found there. Initially, he asked the Lord to spare the city if fifty righteous people were found. The Lord responded with, "If I find fifty righteous people within the city, I will spare the city for their sakes." Abraham then asked if He would spare the city if only forty-five righteous people were found. The Lord responded with, "If I find forty-five righteous people within the city, I will spare the city for their sakes."

Then Abraham asked if He would spare the city if only forty righteous people were found. The Lord responded with, "If I find forty righteous people within the city, I will spare the city for their sakes." Then Abraham asked if He would spare the city if only thirty righteous people where there. The Lord responded with, "If I find thirty righteous people within the city, I will spare the city for their sakes." Abraham again asked the Lord if He would spare the city if twenty righteous people were found. The Lord responded with, "If I find twenty righteous people within the city, I will spare the city for their sakes." Asking one more time, Abraham pleaded with Him to not destroy the city if ten righteous people were found. The Lord responded with, "If I find ten righteous people within the city, I will spare the city for their sakes." What we see in this is the Lord kept telling Abraham that He would spare the city, even though this was a wicked city. Yet the Lord heard the prayer of one righteous man. Unfortunately, there were not ten righteous people found in the city. *Genesis 18*

From this we learn to stand in repentance for our loved ones, and pray bold, specific prayers for them, for the Lord hears your prayer.

All these examples show that if one person stands in the gap and repents for the sins of another, the mercy and forgiveness of God can be won on their behalf, avoiding the judgment of God. Consequences for sin will still have to be paid. But with one standing in the gap for another's sin, the mercy of God can be released, lessening the deserved punishment. None of us receive exactly what we deserve. We deserve death and eternal damnation. But with Jesus' sacrifice on the cross, He took upon Himself the harsh, cruel consequences of sin so we could go free. Our punishment for sin does not compare to what it would have been for us if Jesus had not taken our sins upon Himself.

Jesus, Our Ultimate Example

Sin causes a break in our relationship with God. Jesus paid the price for us and took our penalty of sin upon Himself. When we were stuck in our sin, deceived by life's choices, entangled in a web of rebellion; we were prisoners of war and stuck in the enemy's grip.

Jesus came and did for us what we could not do for ourselves. Jesus stood in the gap for us.

He said, *"Father, forgive them they know not what they do." Luke 23:34*

He stood in the gap for our sins, our rebellion, and our deception and said, "Father, forgive them." He had no sin of His own, yet He asked the Father to forgive His persecutors. There was a condition that needed to be met. Jesus met it. He left us His example to follow after Him.

Just like Jesus, Stephen prayed for those who were stoning him to death in *Acts 7:60*. He prayed, *"Lord, do not charge them with this sin."*

He was unjustly stoned to death, a human being like you and I. Yet he prayed as Jesus prayed.

Their prayers were effective. Their prayers caused confusion in the kingdom of Hell.

Jesus made a way for us to be free from Satan's control and enter into His abundant eternal life. He is our example. We can stand in the gap for our children and ask the Lord to forgive them from their sin. This is a powerful strategy that often gets overlooked. It carries significant weight in preventing the impending judgment off your kids.

While we cannot save anyone from damnation, we can be used by God to bring His mercy and forgiveness in their lives.

How to Stand in the Gap

For each kid found in sin, insert his/her name in the prayer and use this as a starting point. Once you stand in the gap, you need to break the curse that was set in motion by their sin. The Holy Spirit will lead you in a prayer to fit your specific situation. Be led by the Holy Spirit, but do not neglect to stand in the gap for your kids. They desperately need you to do so. In order to simplify this prayer, I used "He." You can change it to fit your child.

Prayer:

Father, I stand in the gap for my child and ask for forgiveness for his sin.

Forgive (name), for he knows not what he does. Forgive him for how he caused You pain and grant him pardon.

Open his eyes to the truth and give him a willing heart to fall upon Your mercy and repent.

I break, cancel, and reverse every negative word directed to him. I break the power of every curse directed to him, regardless if he or someone else spoke it. I ask for forgiveness for those word curses, Lord.

Devil, I come against you and bind your power now. I command any demonic assignments released against my child to be broken, stripped of power and all assignments destroyed in Jesus' name. Your assignments are null and void here. Leave my child alone! He is forgiven in the name of Jesus.

Father, I forgive (name) for the poor choices he has made and for how it affected me. I forgive him for the pain and shame that it caused me. Father, I forgive him for disappointing me. I choose to release him to You. I let go of all the bound up emotions. Forgive me for the judgments in my heart against him.

Father, I apply the blood of Jesus on (name) life. Devil, you can't have him because the blood has been applied. Be removed from him now in the name of Jesus. Amen.

Death Angel

Just as the death angel bypassed the homes with the applied blood, the devil sees your spiritual act of applying Jesus' blood over your kids, and it becomes harder for him to ransack their lives.

Ask the Holy Spirit how much and how long to stand in the gap for them in forgiveness.

Moses stood in the gap and asked the Lord to pardon the iniquity of the Israelites.

Pardon the iniquity of this people, I pray, according to the greatness of your mercy, just as You have forgiven this people from Egypt even until now. Then the Lord said: I have pardoned, according to your word. Numbers 14:19 & 20

Moses understood this principle. According to his intercession for Israel, God granted him his request. Your intercession for your kids is heard in Heaven. God is not a respecter of persons. What He did for Moses, He will do for you.

What He did for Elijah, He will do for you.

His word says in *James 5:17 & 18 Elijah was a man with a nature like ours, and he prayed earnestly that is would not rain; and it did not rain on the land for three years and six months. And he prayed again, and the heaven gave rain and the earth produced its fruit.*

Elijah prayed earnestly. He stood in the gap. God heard his prayer and responded.

The Lord hears your prayer and will respond.

The effective, fervent prayer of a righteous man avails much. *James 5:16*

In Review

- Standing in the gap means doing for someone what he cannot or will not do for himself at this point in time.

- Unconfessed and unrepented sin gives the devil a legal right in your children's lives.

- Standing in the gap must be carried out or the demonic strategy against their life will overtake them.

- Jesus stood in the gap asking the Father to forgive His persecutors for He said they know not what they do.

- We must pray on behalf of our kids and repent for their sins so the enemy of their soul does not completely overtake them.

There may come a point in time when the Lord may say, "Enough! Put them on the altar." It's time for them to experience the consequences of their prolonged stubborn choices. In the next chapter, we will discuss what you are to do when God says, "Enough!"

Chapter Five

STRATEGY FIVE: THE POWER OF SURRENDER

"Enough is enough! Put them on the altar and trust Me."

These were the sobering words I heard the Lord speak to me—not exactly what I wanted to hear. Yet I knew that as I did what He asked of me and trusted Him, He would work all things out for good, for He will not violate His word.

There may come a point in time when the Lord says, "Put them on My altar." Your faith will be challenged to the most extreme measures. While it may be hard to place the kids you carried in your womb on the altar, obedience to the Lord is key. As the ultimate test of your surrender, the Lord might ask you to put them on the altar even though this may mean their lives may be required.

Yet, you must put God first and foremost and not let your kids become an idol in your life. Anything you hold onto, look up to, or desire more than the Lord can easily become an idol in your life. Your kids are no exception. So, despite the love you have for your kids, you must show that you love God first and willingly put them on the altar.

Your kids have free will, but free will is not free. It is costly.

When they continue to resist and rebel—in spite of your prayers for them, in spite of all the counsel you've given, in spite of all the correction and discipline they have received—they are choosing to allow free will to bring a heavy price in their lives.

Though God is merciful and long-suffering, He is also just.

He gives us so many chances to turn our hearts away from evil and do good. He gives us many chances to repent from our own selfish ways and choose His ways.

Unfortunately, their poor choices do not only affect them.

This is not an easy road to walk. When they resist and rebel, they are rebelling against God. They are setting themselves up for destruction. That destruction is painful not only for them but for all involved.

Life isn't fair, but God is always just.

Put them on the altar of God and don't keep picking them back up. Don't continue rescuing them from all their mess-ups. Let them feel the consequences of their poor choices.

Relinquish control. Abraham put Isaac on the altar, not because of rebellion, but as an act of total surrender and obedience to the Lord. In his care, God supernaturally supplied the sacrifice, and at the last moment, the Lord stopped Abraham.

The Lord is not asking you to literally put your kids on an altar, but instead to release control in your heart and verbally, in prayer, give them to Him. He is asking you to resolve in your heart that regardless of what happens to them, you will trust God and serve Him all the days of your life. He is asking you to radically trust Him.

Radical Obedience

I had to do this with most of my loved ones. It was difficult at first, but it was even more difficult to watch them destroy their lives with poor choices.

The fear that bombards your heart can be overwhelming. It is heart wrenching to watch your kids rebel, knowing their lives may be called into account.

In this moment, you may experience a torrential down pour of tears that feel like death, so pour those tears out to your Heavenly Father. When you walk through this type of intense pain, you will see why *Isaiah 54:5* says the Lord is your husband. As you turn to the Lord, His comfort is matched by no other.

The Lord wants to become your husband and comfort you more than anyone else ever could. He must become the one you place your complete hope and trust in. Your relationship with the Lord will reach a height you never knew was possible when you go through such an intense battle and you truly relinquish all to Him.

He is your maker and your Husband, and the comfort He gives cannot compare to any earthly comfort.

His presence and His word will bring you comfort this world knows nothing about.

He Will Carry You Through

Let those who suffer according to the will of God commit their souls to Him in doing good as to a faithful creator. 1 Peter 4:19

You are suffering, but it is according to the will of God. Your comfort is in knowing you are in obedience to His will, and He is so close to you. He will carry you through this. You are never alone.

In prayer commit your own soul to Him again. Commit all your decisions to Him. Commit all your actions to Him. He is faithful and will be faithful to you.

You are suffering for doing good, but the Lord is faithful and will bless you for your obedience and sacrifice to Him.

Radical Prayer:

"Lord, I put my kids on the altar of surrender, and I trust You with them. Do what You need to do to get their attention but save their souls from hell. I trust You no matter what."

Radical lovers of God pray radical prayers and live radically obedient lives unto Him, not because it's easy, but because it's right.

The Altar of Surrender

The altar of surrender is a point of trust for you and a point of refining fire for them.

For you, the altar of surrender requires your complete and ultimate trust in God.

> Will you let go of your control and all the ways you're trying to help them since at this point they don't want the help?

> Will you surrender control to the Lord fully and trust Him regardless of the cost?

> Will you say yes to whatever the Lord may require of you?

> Will you trust the Lord will all your heart, all your soul, all your will, and all

your strength and not hold anything back?

Jesus wants your full surrender. Trust Him with your children. Trust Him with your heart. It is in these times, you must cling to the word of God and like Esther, pray, "Lord, if I perish I perish." It is important to pray as Esther prayed and completely trust in the Lord for your kids.

Trust in the Lord with all your heart, and lean not on your own understanding. In all your ways acknowledge Him, and He shall direct your paths. Proverbs 3:5 & 6

The Altar of Refining Fire

For your kids, this altar is an altar of refining fire.

As the heat in their lives gets turned up, will they soften their hearts and repent? When their poor choices began to bring harsh consequences, will they humble themselves and turn to God? His mercy is new every moment. It is not His will for them to perish. Will they persist and rebel? In so doing, they will be devoured by the sword, the sword of their own poor choices.

During my kids' trial by fire, I cried out to the Lord. I needed to hear from Him, for the fear that was trying to grip my heart was intense.

I was desperate to hear the word of the Lord, for my mother's heart was in turmoil. Everything was out of control. I had already surrendered my kids on the altar. I felt like everything was out of my reach now. I awoke at 4 am and went to spend time with the Lord. "Lord, I have to hear from You." Speak to me from Your word."

I opened my Bible to a scripture I do not even remember reading though I have read through the Bible many times.

There it was, an unfamiliar scripture, staring at me. It seemed to jump off the page like a neon light.

Thus says the Lord: Refrain your voice from weeping, and your eyes from tears; for your work shall be rewarded, says the Lord, and they shall come back from the land of the enemy. There is hope in your future, says the Lord, that your children shall come back to their own border. Jeremiah 31:16 & 17

That was all I needed! His word jumped off that page, and I knew it was Him speaking hope to my heart.

I knew He was with me and would work this out. My hope was renewed in a moment. I hung on to this word every time my heart wanted to sink in despair. Every time I felt my spirit getting low, I remembered the word of the Lord, and it brought me strength and hope.

His word brings hope. His word brings comfort. His word brings deliverance.

Keep this scripture in the forefront of your heart. Your work will be rewarded says the Lord.

Regardless of how desperate your situation seems, remember God is greater.

He wants to do the same for you. He wants to mark your life with such a significant print you will never be the same. As you go through the fire, your faith will rise to a height you did not know was possible, and the devil will know you are more dangerous now for having survived the fiery trial.

Nothing is impossible for those who believe.

Prayer to Release Your Kids on the Altar of the Lord:

Father, I come in agreement with the word of God, and in the name of Jesus I pray. I come before Your throne and lay my requests before You.

Father, You sent Your Son to the cross and took all my failures, all my success, all my works, all my sin, all my hidden motives, all that is obvious and all that is not, and You died for it all. You took upon Yourself what was meant for me. Father, thank You for sending Your beloved Son to die in my place so I can enjoy Your presence now and for eternity.

Lord, today I lay my burdens at the foot of the cross. I acknowledge that I have been carrying a weight that was not meant for me to carry. I commit to You all my fears, worries, and all that causes me to strive and leave Your presence. I thank You for forgiving me and setting me free from guilt, worry, shame, bitterness, lack of forgiveness, and trying to control my kids. I thank You for forgiving me from all that separates me from You.

Now, I lift my eyes to Your throne of mercy and grace. I receive your mercy and grace today. I receive your ability to thrive in life even if things don't go the way I wished they would. I release control of my kids, and I give them to You, faithful Father. I lay them at Your altar, Lord, and I trust You with my kids. Father, according to Your word in *Philippians 2:13*, work in their lives and cause them to both will and do according to Your good purpose.

I align myself with your Word: *Commit your way to the Lord, trust also in Him, and He shall bring it to pass. Psalm 37:5*

Father, I commit all my work into Your hands, and You will bring to pass what is of You, not what is of me.

Commit your works to the Lord, and your thoughts will be established. Proverbs 16:3

Father, I commit my works to You, and You will help me line my thoughts up to be pleasing in Your sight. My thoughts are established, set securely by the Lord of Lord because I have committed all my work unto Him.

Father, I commit my soul (my mind, will and emotions) to You. If I must suffer for the Gospel, then so be it. I will be surrendered unto Your will, and You will redeem me by Your Spirit.

I choose to line up and be obedient unto You. I will not please man but God first and foremost. My children are accountable to You. Lord, I will pray for them according to Your Word that tells us to pray and never give up. I will not fret about their choices because You, Oh Lord, are able to redeem men from the oppression of the enemy and from their own stubborn, rebellious hearts.

I bless what You have done in my heart today, and I bless what You are doing in my kid's hearts. I choose to rejoice in all things giving thanks to You, my redeemer and my friend. In Jesus' Name I pray, Amen.

If you just prayed this prayer and placed your kids on the altar, know that this is not the end. You may need to pray this over a few times as you release all the pent up fears. Allow the Holy Spirit time to heal your heart as you pray. This time in prayer is vital to your standing in the gap for your kids. Don't rush this prayer. Expand it to fit your needs.

In Review

- The Lord is not asking you to literally put your kids on an altar, but instead to release control in your heart and verbally, in prayer, give them to Him.

- Placing your kids on the altar of surrender may be the hardest thing He ever asks you to do.

- Radical obedience is not for the faint of heart but for those who mean business with God, those who are truly sold out and committed to Him.

- Radical lovers of God pray radical prayers and live radically obedient lives unto Him, not because it's easy, but because it's right.

- The altar of surrender for you is the altar of refining fire for them.

- Pray and release control of your kids and trust God. He loves them more than you.

Things are shifting in the spirit realm because there is a war in the Heavens. Change is beginning to take place. It is time to take your radical obedience and do something radical with it. Something that will confuse and confound the devil and break open the prison gate. We will discuss this powerful strategy in the next chapter.

Chapter Six

STRATEGY SIX: THE POWER OF PRAISE

GET UP! AND DANCE! ON THE FACE OF YOUR ENEMY!

Sometimes situations will seem to become worse before they become better. Although I had surrendered my kids in prayer on the altar of the Lord and trusted Him with their lives, the circumstances still turned from bad to worse. An avalanche of fear was bombarding my heart again. I was beside myself. There was nothing I could do to change these situations, and I tried, trust me.

I sat there, slipping into despair and despondency, for my best efforts seemed to fail again.

Instantly, I heard the voice of the Lord speak to me. "Get up! And Dance! On The Face Of Your Enemy! It was so loud and so strong, almost as if it were an audible voice. There was no mistaking it.

It was the last thing I felt like doing, but in obedience, I pushed myself to respond, and my spirit quickly came into agreement. I knew it was the voice of the Lord, for during this whole season my ability to hear His voice grew insurmountably. I got up from that place of sorrow and danced all over the house. Understanding the power of praise, I knew I needed to put it into action at this time regardless of how I felt. I got up and began jumping and leaping and shouting and praising God. I continued to declare out loud, "My kids see the light and will return to Christ!"

I was making a declaration with every step, and I knew it. My actions were confusing and confounding the vindictive plan of the enemy! I knew with every step, I was stomping on his plans. I was stomping on his face. With every step I took, I could feel my authority rising. I was destroying his assignments with my heart-felt praise!

Strategy number six is to dance on the face of your enemy! Let your praise be loud and let it shake the heavens. Arise in the midst of your problems with your kids and begin to praise the

Lord. Shift your focus and attention from the problem to His beautiful presence. He alone can rescue your kids from any and every horrible situation they may be in at the moment. Turning your attention and affection to Him will release the power of praise in your household.

The strategies of the Lord don't always make sense, but they are always perfect. He never fails us.

The power of praise is a mystery, but it works. It defied the enemy and confused his plans. Many times in battle, God first sent His people in to praise, and the enemy turned against themselves.

Praise Will Destroy Those Barriers Against You

- In *Acts 16*, Paul and Silas were thrown in jail for casting out a demon from a slave girl. The multitude rose up against them and had them thrown in jail. But at midnight, they were praying and singing hymns to God. The Lord caused an earthquake to shake open the prison doors and everyone's chains were loosed. The keeper of the prison and his whole family received salvation!

- The Lord told Jehoshaphat and all of Judah to sing and praise the Lord in the face of the enemy's attack. *2 Chronicles 20* The Lord set ambushes against their enemies and the enemies defeated each other.

Praise brought a victorious end to all involved! Prison doors were opened, shackles fell off, enemies turned on themselves in confusion, all because God's people praised in their darkest hour!

Your praise will confuse your enemy and confound his plan!

Your praise is your strength. It's supernatural, not just in shifting your mood but in causing circumstances to change. It's one of the mysteries of God. But we must make our flesh obey and praise even when it is the last thing we feel like doing. Praise Him when your heart is gripped with wrenching pain, hopelessness, and fear.

I continued to obey all the strategies the Lord taught me. Slowly, one by one, victory was happening as each child started returning to his senses, out of the bondage of sin, and out of the demonic hold of the enemy.

Your family may be going through a wicked, demonic attack. It will feel like insurmountable pressure. In these overwhelming times, don't look at their sin, look beyond the sin and look to Jesus.

Trust the Lord with your kids. He loves them more than you.

Rise up in the midst of your circumstance and tell the devil, "Devil, you can't have my kids!" Mean it when you say it. They belong to the Lord. Release your praise unto the Lord and you will confuse the devil and frustrate his plans.

The Lord will grant that the enemies who rise up against you will be defeated before you. They will come at you from one direction but flee from you in seven.
Deuteronomy 28:7

Out of the ashes arose a warrior. After the demonic ambush, I became the devil's worst nightmare, and so can you.

Let your life be a highway for the Lord to walk on. As you seek Him and obey His voice, He will cause your enemy to be defeated before you.

This season of testing has marked me and changed my life forever. I can truly say death has no hold on me. I've been though the fire and met the lover of my soul. He radically changed me. I shall never be moved.

I have set the Lord always before me; Because He is at my right hand I shall not be moved. Psalm 16:8

In Review

- Praise destroys the enemy's plans.

- Jehoshaphat, Paul and Silas, are two Biblical examples where praise defeated the enemy's assignment.

- Praise will not just shift your mood, but it will cause circumstances to change.

- It's one of the mysteries of God.

- The strategies of the Lord don't always make sense, but they are always perfect.

Use these strategies and make that devil flee from your lives. Now it's your turn to take what you know and make some adjustments. What has the Lord spoken to your heart as you have read this book? In what ways have you felt faith rise up in you?

Your kids are one of the most cherished gifts the Lord has given you. Every parent wants their kids to succeed. Love them. Encourage them. Stand with them. Fight for them. Remember the Lord loves them and wants them to succeed even more than you. In the next chapter, we will talk about your plan of action.

Chapter Seven

CONCLUSION: MAKE YOUR PLAN

How Do We Keep What We Have Learned?

- By remembering Whose you are!

  o You are a blood bought son or daughter of the Most High God.

- By remembering who Jesus is.

  o He is the all powerful, all knowing and ever present King of Kings and Lord of Lords.

  o He rose triumphantly over sin, the grave, and the devil.

- Recognize the real enemy, the devil, and declare war on his plan of destruction, which is against you and your family.

We fight the warfare coming against us by standing on His word.

- **So shall they fear the name of the Lord from the west and His glory from the rising of the sun. When the enemy shall come in like a flood, <u>the Spirit of the Lord shall lift up a standard against him.</u>**
  Isaiah 59:19

This means that you will have times of enemy downpour. It will seem like EVERYTHING is falling apart. BUT it is in these times we must remember . . . <u>the Spirit of the Lord shall lift up a standard against him.</u>

To "Lift up a standard against him" is literally to put to flight, to chase away to cause to flee!!

So when you are facing a battle, it is your job to put the devil in his place. It is your job to partner with the word of the Lord and put the enemy to flight and release God's word in every situation.

Prayer

Devil, you may try to come against me and my family with spears and swords, but I come against you in the Name of

the Lord Almighty. You may try to come against us like a flood, but the Spirit of the Lord shall lift up a standard against you, put you to flight, and cause you to flee. You are defeated devil, in Jesus name.

It's your turn now. You need to create your road map, your God-given strategy. Get into the presence of God and ask Him for revelation on these strategies. Make them your own.

The Lord wants to speak to you and give you a tailor-made road map for your kids. Use these strategies and add to them as He directs you. He truly has a plan and will not disappoint you.

For I know the thoughts that I think towards you, says the Lord, thoughts of peace and not of evil, to give you a future and a hope. Jeremiah 29:11

Be encouraged. The Lord will guide you. He will show you your kids' hearts and exactly what sins they need to be called out of and exactly how to do it.

Be patient through it all. This is a marathon—not a sprint.

Do you not know that in a race, all the runners run, but only one gets the prize? Run in such a way as to get the prize. **1 Corinthians 9:24**

Run your race. Don't look at others and let them discourage you. In a race, everyone has a lane. Stay in your own lane. Run your own race.

Most importantly, stay in the presence of God and keep your peace. Your well-being is most important. It will keep you strong and healthy, so you can be all God has called you to be.

Therefore, caretaker, take care of yourself. Stay filled with God's love or you won't make it. The enemy hates you because you are the obstacle that stops him from completely destroying your kids. So take care of yourself. Your kids need you to stay strong. As your strength is found in Christ, stay in His presence and listen for His voice.

Through all the ups and downs, the Lord is with you. God is growing you through this. *He will work all things together for good for those who love Him and are called according to His purpose.* **Romans 8:28** Purpose will arise from the ashes. Since love always wins in life, allow the Lord to keep filling you with His love, so you have His love to give away.

Don't let the enemy speak lies to your mind. Realize he will try to deceive you if he can. He will discourage you if he can. He will bring fear to you if he can. Don't allow him access to your thoughts. Stop the negative mental tape. You are on a mission. Stay focused and fulfill your assignment.

Jesus is with you and for you. Never forget that.

When the enemy targets your mind, take authority and bind that devil. Don't allow him to cause you to doubt or fear, not even for one day. You are God's chosen agent on a mission. Get your battle gear on and fight the good fight, mighty Christian soldier. Since you have found Christ, you already have all the tools you need to fight this battle and win. Jesus in you is sufficient. The Holy Spirit will direct your every step as you look to Him.

The power of your words, the power of your authority, the power of your affirmation, the power of forgiveness, the power of surrender, and the power of praise are just a few of the strategies the Lord taught me. They are powerful, and they work. Begin today with your commitment to Christ. Choose this day to partner with Him and begin turning this deception around. There is something you can do. Your hands are not tied. Prayer is a mighty weapon in the life of a bold warrior that knows their God-given rights.

These six strategies have been tested and proven true in my life and in the lives of many other believers. So use them. Get up and fight using these divine strategies.

You are in a war, and you've been called to the front lines. Take action with these God-given strategies. Partner with a close friend in prayer, for together the two of you will put to flight an enemy ten thousand. *Deuteronomy 32:30* There is power in praying and standing in agreement with a faith-filled friend. Even if you don't completely follow your plan every day, remember God's word says to get back up, mighty warrior. Don't get discouraged. It is His grace that will lead you anyway.

Though a righteous man falls seven times he will rise again. Proverbs 24:16

For though we walk in the flesh, we do not war according to the flesh. For the weapons of our warfare are not carnal but mighty in God for pulling down strongholds, casting down arguments and every high thing that exalts itself against the knowledge of God, bringing every thought into captivity to the obedience of Christ, and being ready to punish all disobedience when your obedience is fulfilled. 2 Corinthians 10:3–6

In the next chapter I have written a prayer you can use in daily warfare intercession for your kids. Use this prayer and remember to stand in bold authority knowing Christ has given you His authority.

In the final chapter, I have included scriptures to help you stand strong in the Lord regardless of the situation.

Chapter Eight

WARFARE PRAYER TO CALL YOUR LOVED ONES OUT OF DARKNESS

Father, You have already delivered me from the works of darkness; therefore, I have the right to speak to the darkness and tell it what to do. I stand in agreement with the Word of God and declare that Jesus is the head over every power and authority. He has given me authority to trample the works of darkness.

I take back what belongs to me. Devil, you can't have my kids. ***The Kingdom of God suffers violence and the violent take it by force. Matthew 11:12*** I take back by force everything that has been stolen from me.

Father, in the name of Jesus, I take authority over the ruling spirits working against my kids. I stand in agreement with the Spirit of God for the lives of my kids. I bind up the strong man and prohibit him from interfering with this prayer. **Mark 3:27** I render you silenced, muzzled, blinded, and bound.

My enemies will cower before me, and I will trample down their high places. **Deuteronomy 33:29** I trample down every high place of rebellion, pride, and idolatry working against my loved ones. I take the word of the Lord and tear down every high thing that exalts itself above the name of Jesus. I bind every power and principality of rebellion, pride, and idolatry influencing my loved ones and drawing them away from the Lord. I command you to leave them now in Jesus' name. I break your power. I break your curse.

I command the spirits of compromise and complacency to stop influencing them and leave them now in Jesus' name. I command every lying spirit and every spirit of deception working against them to be bound and cast out in Jesus' name. **Mark 16:17**

I bind and gag every demonic spirit influencing my loved ones to sin.

I render you inoperative in their lives. I close every door, every portal, and every access point that was opened to the demonic realm in their lives.

I apply the blood of Jesus over them, and what I decree shall come to pass. *Job 22:28* I decree that all my children will be taught by the Lord and great will be their peace. *Isaiah 54:13*

I speak in faith and am fully persuaded that the word of God will not return unto me void. I declare that my loved ones have died to sin and have been raised in Christ and are now seated in heavenly places. The same Spirit that rose Christ from the dead lives in them, giving life to their mortal bodies. *Romans 8:11*

For every place in their life where they have given up and have become hopeless, I command the spirit of hopelessness and death to leave them now in Jesus' name. I speak resurrection power over them.

I stand in my authority, and I decree over them hope, life, and destiny fulfilled. They are victorious at every turn. They walk in humility with great favor on their lives. They always give glory to God.

I declare that my children walk in the fullness of God and are healed emotionally, physically, and mentally by their heavenly Father.

I declare that **the Son of Righteousness shall arise with healing in His wings** for them. *Malachi 4:2*

Father, let Your Kingdom come, let Your will be done on earth as it is in Heaven. *Matthew 6:10* My loved ones are bold for Christ and are on fire to passionately serve God. They seek Him with all their heart. *Jeremiah 29:13*

Father, surround them with godly influences and remove the wicked ones from their midst. Capture their minds and fill them with the understanding of Your great love. I bind their mind to the mind of Christ. I bind their will to the will of Christ. *Matthew 18:18*

I declare that they are new creatures in Christ, the old has gone, the new has come. *2 Corinthians 5:17* This day, all of heaven hears. This day, all of heaven responds: my lineage is built upon the solid rock. I decree that Jesus is the way maker, the giver of life, and the victorious King over my family.

I decree that my descendants walk in obedience to Christ and serve Him all the days of their lives. They have been rescued from the kingdom of darkness and brought into the kingdom of light. *Colossians 1:13*

I decree that my family is reconciled and restored back to God's original design.

Now Father, I ask You to release warring angels to war against any resistant demons and release the fire of God against them and destroy every work of darkness attacking my loved ones now in Jesus' name I pray. Amen.

Chapter 9

SCRIPTURES TO DAILY PRAY OVER YOUR KIDS

God's word will never return unto you void. Make His word part of your everyday life. Begin to speak His word in the lives of your loved ones and watch as God takes His word and begins molding and shaping your kid's hearts. He is faithful to His word. It is your privilege to speak God's word.

Don't let anyone tell you His word does not work. It works. It already worked, as He created the world by His spoken word. Below are some scriptures you can use, as you become that wall of defense against the onslaughts of the enemy who wants to steal the hearts and lives of your kids.

Rise up in faith and walk in your dominion. Don't let the devil take from you what God said is yours. Arise, mighty warrior in Christ, and destroy the devil's agenda. You can tear down his plans and wreak havoc on his plans. Be aggressive in your prayers. You have the Kingdom of Heaven on your side. God will never fail you. He is always with you. He always rewards obedience to His word.

God's Word:

I am watching over My words to perform it. Jeremiah 1:12

The angels harken unto the word of the Lord and do His will. Psalm 103:20

I am the Lord who carries out the words of his servants and fulfills the predictions of his messengers. Isaiah 44:26

You will declare a thing, and it will be established for you. Job 22:28

My Words:

This is the confidence we have in approaching God: That if we ask anything according to His will, He hears us. And if we know He hears us, we know we have what we have asked. 1 John 5:14

You can have what you say if you believe and do not doubt. Mark 11:23

Faith:

But without faith, it is impossible to please Him. For those who come to God must believe that He is and that He is a rewarder of those who diligently seek Him. Hebrews 11:6

God's Love:

Now may the Lord direct your hearts into the love of God and into the patience of Christ. 2 Thessalonians 3:5

For Your hope does not disappoint, because the love of God has been pour out in their hearts by the Holy Spirit. Romans 5:5

For You love them with an unending love, You said, I am persuaded that neither death nor life, nor angels nor principalities nor powers, nor things present nor things to come, nor height nor depth nor any other created thing, shall be able to separate us from the love of God which is in Christ Jesus our Lord. Romans 8:38 & 39

But God demonstrated His own love towards us, in that while we were still sinners, Christ died for us. Romans 5:8

Perseverance:

That they would consider it pure joy whenever they face trials of many kinds because they know that the testing of their faith develops perseverance. Perseverance must finish its work so that they may be mature and complete, not lacking anything. James 1: 2–4

Will:

For it is God who works in you both to will and do for His good pleasure. Philippians 2:13

And we have this confidence in the Lord concerning you, both that you do and will do the things we command you. Now may the Lord direct your hearts into the love of God and into the patience of Christ. 2 Thessalonians 3:4 & 5

Call:

Call unto me in the day of trouble and I will deliver you and you shall honor and glorify me. Psalm 50:15

Lead:

I will instruct you and teach you in the way you should go: I will counsel you and watch over you. Psalm 32:8

Grace:

My grace is sufficient for you, for My strength is made perfect in weakness. 2 Corinthians 12:9

Conquerors:

In all these things we are more than conquerors through Him who loved us.
Romans 8:37

Mind:

Do not conform any longer to the pattern of this world, but be transformed by the renewing of your mind that you may prove what is that good and acceptable and perfect will of God. Romans 12: 2

Take every thought captive and make it obedient to Christ. 2 Corinthians 10:5

Peace:

Great peace have they who love Your law and nothing can make them stumble. Psalm 119:165

For You will keep him in perfect peace who's mind is stayed on You, because he trusts in You. Isaiah 26:3

All your children shall be taught by the Lord, and great shall be the peace of your children. Isaiah 54:13

Direct Them:

Direct their footsteps according to your word; let no sin rule over them. Redeem them from the oppression of men, that they may obey your precepts. Make Your face shine on them and teach them Your decrees. Psalm 119:133–135

CONTACT INFORMATION

Cathy Coppola is an ordained pastor and a married mother of four adult children. She is the founder and president of Cathy Coppola International Ministries. She teaches the word of God and moves in signs and wonders. Her mandate is to preach the word of God by the power of the Holy Spirit, and release miracles, signs and wonders to the nations.

She has ministered in the United States, South America and Africa teaching the word of God, praying for the sick, and casting out demons.

She can be seen on
The Holy Spirit Broadcasting Network &
ROKU.

Her program is called,
Where The Fire Meets The Clouds.
You can watch her at
HSBN.tv (www.bit.ly/25txOHx) and ROKU
(www.ROKU.com)

Her previous book titled
From Grief to Glory
is available at her website, cathycoppola.org or
on Amazon (www.amazon.com/From-Grief-
To-Glory-Adversity/dp/1931820287)

For More Information Visit:
Cathy Coppola International Ministries at
cathycoppola.org

Or write to:
Cathy Coppola International Ministries
P.O. Box 2923
Mission Viejo, California 92692

1-855-583-6767
info@cathycoppola.org

You can also connect with her on her
YouTube channel (www.bit.ly/1RMjRjK)
and her Facebook page
(http://bit.ly/1RvRYdV)

OTHER BOOKS BY CATHY COPPOLA

From Grief To Glory

www.amazon.com/From-Grief-To-Glory-Adversity/dp/1931820287

Every adversity in your life is an opportunity for you to rise above it and enter into the glorious presence of God, where His love will transform you in ways you never knew were possible. This eight-week devotional will walk you through steps that will engage your heart and ignite in you a radically contagious Christian walk. You will rise above your place of pain and enter into His presence where the glory of God will surround you, and you will be changed forever.

From The Fire Of Adversity To The Fire Of His Love

FROM
Grief
TO
Glory

CATHY COPPOLA

Made in the USA
San Bernardino, CA
01 June 2016